SandCastle 2

More Blends

dr

Pam Scheunemann

Publishing Company

Published by SandCastle™, an imprint of ABDO Publishing Company, 4940 Viking Drive, Edina, Minnesota 55435.

Printed in the United States.

Cover and interior photo credits: Comstock, Corbis Images, Digital Vision, PhotoDisc, Rubberball Productions, Stockbyte

Library of Congress Cataloging-in-Publication Data

Scheunemann, Pam 1955-
　　　Dr / Pam Scheunemann.
　　　　　p. cm. -- (Blends)
　　　ISBN 1-57765-448-X
　　　　　1. Readers (Primary) [1. English language--Phonetics.] I. Title. II. Blends (Series)

PE1119 .S43514 2001
428.1--dc21

00-056562

The SandCastle concept, content, and reading method have been reviewed and approved by a national advisory board including literacy specialists, librarians, elementary school teachers, early childhood education professionals, and parents.

Let Us Know

After reading the book, SandCastle would like you to tell us your stories about reading. What is your favorite page? Was there something hard that you needed help with? Share the ups and downs of learning to read. We want to hear from you! To get posted on the ABDO Publishing Company Web site, send us email at:

sandcastle@abdopub.com

About SandCastle™

Nonfiction books for the beginning reader

- Basic concepts of phonics are incorporated with integrated language methods of reading instruction. Most words are short, and phrases, letter sounds, and word sounds are repeated.

- Readability is determined by the number of words in each sentence, the number of characters in each word, and word lists based on curriculum frameworks.

- Full-color photography reinforces word meanings and concepts.

- "Words I Can Read" list at the end of each book teaches basic elements of grammar, helps the reader recognize the words in the text, and builds vocabulary.

- Reading levels are indicated by the number of flags on the castle.

Look for more SandCastle books in these three reading levels:

Level 1 (one flag)	**Level 2** (two flags)	**Level 3** (three flags)

Grades Pre-K to K 5 or fewer words per page	**Grades K to 1** 5 to 10 words per page	**Grades 1 to 2** 10 to 15 words per page

dr

Drew loves to dream
about fun things to do.

dr

Drake likes to draw with the kids in his class.

dr

Drusi is careful not to drip on her dress.

dr

Andre likes to drive in his toy car.

dr

Andrea and her mom have matching party dresses.

dr

Adrian knows how to swim.

He will not drown.

dr

Sandra drifts off to sleep.

She is dreaming.

dr

Andrew feels bad.

He dropped the plant
while playing.

dr

What are Kendra and her friends doing?

(drinking)

Words I Can Read

Nouns

A noun is a person, place, or thing

car (KAR) p. 11

class (KLASS) p. 7

dress (DRESS) p. 9

milk (MILK) p. 21

mom (MOM) p. 13

plant (PLANT) p. 19

Plural Nouns

A plural noun is more than one person, place, or thing

dresses (DRESS-ez) p. 13

friends (FRENDZ) p. 21

kids (KIDZ) p. 7

things (THINGZ) p. 5

Proper Nouns

A proper noun is the name of a person, place, or thing

Adrian (AY-dree-uhn) p. 15

Andre (AHN-dray) p. 11

Andrea (AHN-dree-uh) p. 13

Andrew (AN-droo) p. 19

Drake (DRAKE) p. 7

Drew (DROO) p. 5

Drusi (DROO-see) p. 9

Kendra (KEN-druh) p. 21

Sandra (SAN-druh) p. 17

22

Verbs

A verb is an action or being word

are (AR) p. 21
do (DOO) p. 5
doing (DOO-ing) p. 21
draw (DRAW) p. 7
dream (DREEM) p. 5
dreaming (DREEM-ing)
  p. 17
drifts (DRIFTSS) p. 17
drinking (DRINGK-ing)
  p. 21
drip (DRIP) p. 9
drive (DRIVE) p. 11

dropped (DROPT) p. 19
drown (DROUN) p. 15
feels (FEELZ) p. 19
have (HAV) p. 13
is (IZ) pp. 9, 17
knows (NOHZ) p. 15
likes (LIKESS) pp. 7, 11
loves (LUHVZ) p. 5
playing (PLAY-ing) p. 19
sleep (SLEEP) p. 17
swim (SWIM) p. 15
will (WIL) p. 15

Adjectives

An adjective describes something

bad (BAD) p. 19
careful (KAIR-fuhl) p. 9
fun (FUHN) p. 5
her (HUR) pp. 9, 13, 21
his (HIZ) pp. 7, 11

matching (MACH-ing)
  p. 13
off (AWF) p. 17
party (PAR-tee) p. 13
toy (TOI) p. 11

23

Match these dr Words
to the Pictures

drum

drink

dresser

drill